What I Look Like When I Am Happy

Heidi Johansen

The Rosen Publishing Group's
PowerStart Press™
New York

For Daniel Ernesto

Published in 2004 by The Rosen Publishing Group, Inc.
29 East 21st Street, New York, NY 10010

First Edition

Book Design: Kim Sonsky
Photo Credits: All photos by Maura B. McConnell.

Library of Congress Cataloging-in-Publication Data

Johansen, Heidi Leigh.
What I look like when I am happy / Heidi Leigh Johansen.
    p. cm. — (Let's look at feelings)
Includes index.
Summary: Describes how different parts of the face look when a person is happy.
  ISBN 1-4042-2506-4
1. Happiness in children—Juvenile literature. [1. Happiness. 2. Facial expression.] I. Title. II. Series.
  BF723.H37J64 2004
  152.4'2–dc21

                                                    2003005985

Manufactured in the United States of America

Contents

I am happy.

My mouth makes a smile
when I am happy.

When I am happy I smile with my mouth closed.

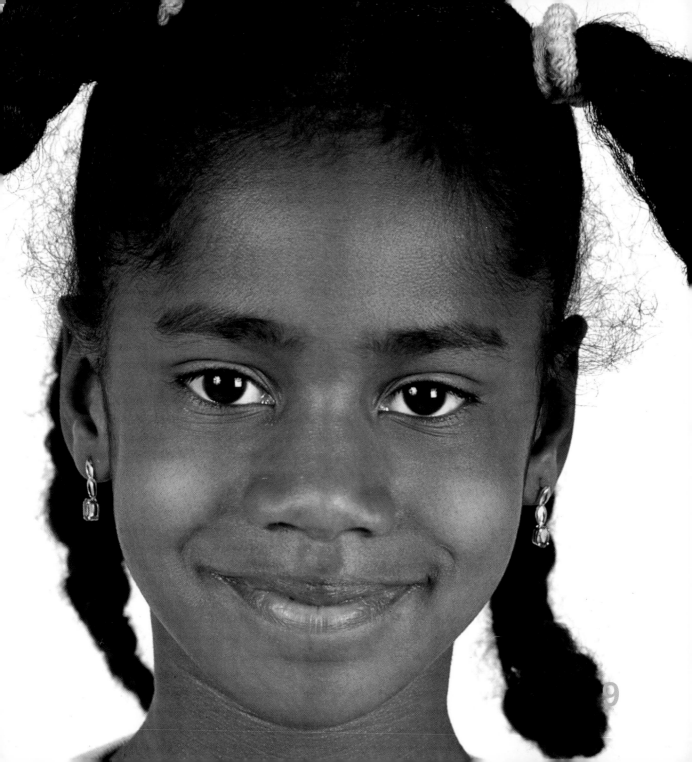
9

You can see my teeth when
I am happy.

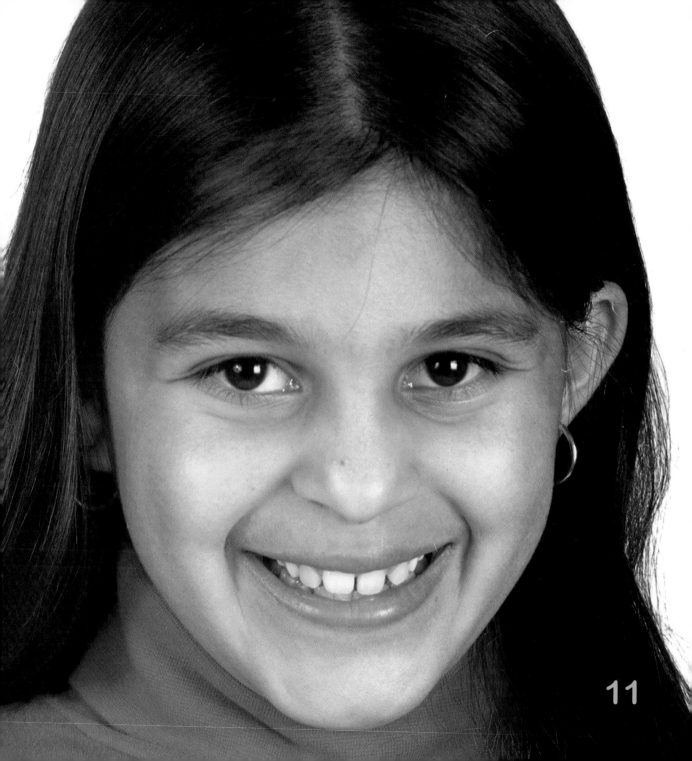

I laugh when I am happy.

13

When I am happy my cheeks look round.

There are lines on both sides of my mouth when I am happy.

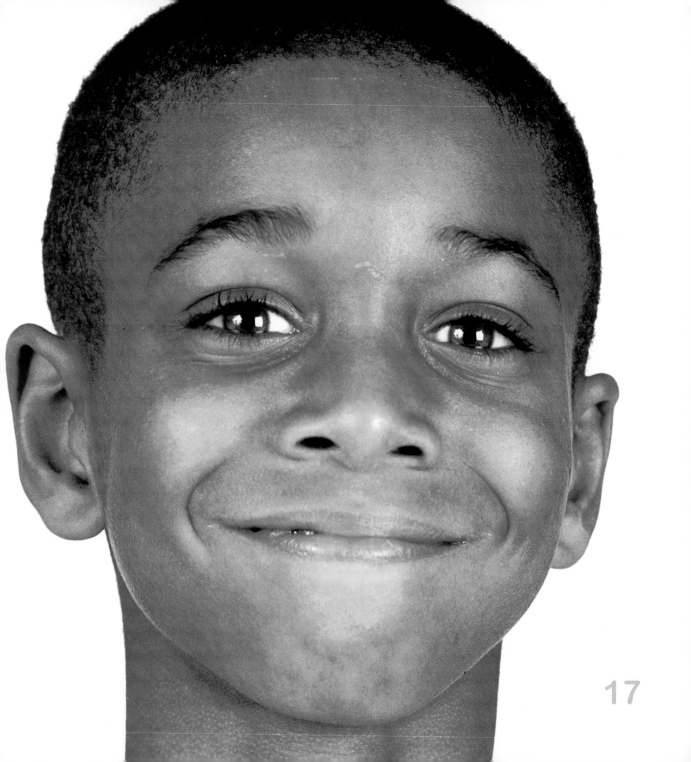

There are lines by my eyes
when I am happy.

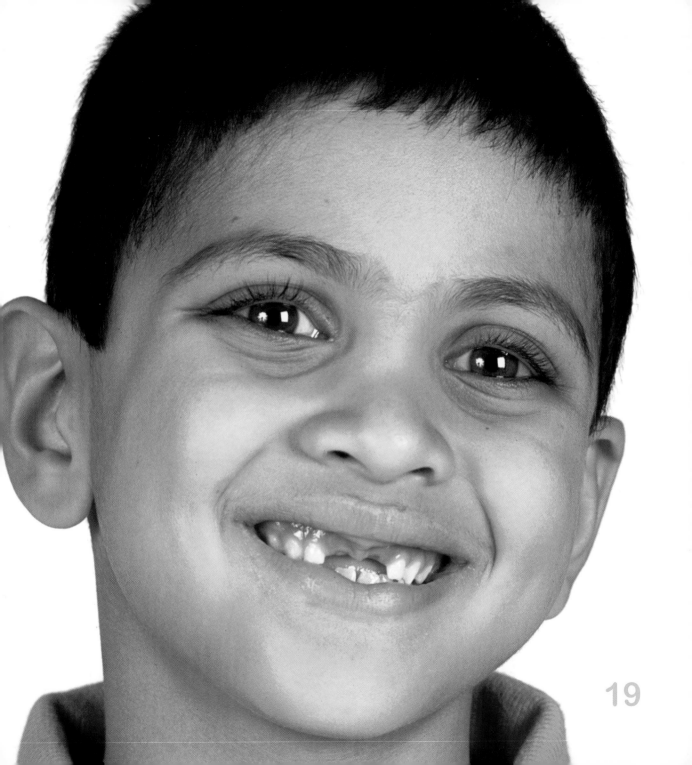

19

There are lines on my nose
when I am happy.

This is what I look like when
I am happy.

23

Words to Know

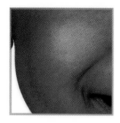

cheek

laugh

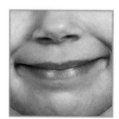

mouth

nose

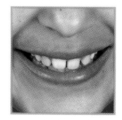

smile

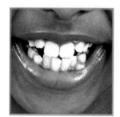

teeth

Index

Web Sites

Due to the changing nature of Internet links, PowerKids Press has developed an online list of Web sites related to the subject of this book. This site is updated regularly. Please use this link to access the list:

www.powerkidslinks.com/llafe/happy/